SPECIAL IN MOVIES

Illustrated with photographs

SPECIAL EFFECTS AND TV

SHAARON COSNER

Julian Messner
New York

Manufactured in the United States of America

Design by Beverly Grace Haw Leung, A Good Thing, Inc.

Library of Congress Cataloging in Publication Data.

Cosner, Shaaron.
  Special effects in TV and movies.

  Includes index.
  Summary: Explores the world of special effects in
television and film, including special props, filming
techniques, atmospheric effects, and experiments that
can be done at home.
  1. Cinematography—Special effects—Juvenile
literature. 2. Television broadcasting—Special effects—
Juvenile literature. [1. Cinematography—Special effects.
2. Television—Special effects] I. Title.
TR858.C67   1985   791.43′024   85-282
ISBN 0-671-46136-2

To Jennifer, Michelle, Nikki,
and Steve Jr.

Photo Credits

ACKNOWLEDGEMENTS

My Thanks to:
Bill Barnett, Los Palmas Productions;

KCET, Public Television for Southern California;

Animation Production of America;

Walt Disney Productions

MESSNER BOOKS BY
SHAARON COSNER

Special Effects in Movies and TV

Be Your Own Weather Forecaster

CONTENTS

A flying dinosaur from *The Land that Time Forgot.*

1

THE WORLD OF SPECIAL EFFECTS

Where else but in the movies or on television can we see a helpless animal sinking into quicksand, a dinosaur attacking a caveman or a spaceship plummeting through a galaxy to save the heroine? The people who make the magic of these scenes are the special effects men. They know that the quicksand is plain old oatmeal in a vat with a false bottom, the giant prehistoric monsters are really three-foot models, and the spaceship is flying over black velvet sprinkled with baking sugar crystals. It's all illusion.

When moving pictures were first invented, there was very little plot and movie makers relied heavily on special effects to keep the audience interested. Thomas Edison made a one-minute film in 1893 called *The Execution of Mary Queen of Scots*. The film showed the queen's head rolling off the chopping block into the dust. The audience was horrified—but came back for more!

George Méliès, a magician, thrilled his audience at the turn of the century when he made a film that showed people flying through the air and disappearing. Today's viewers would probably realize that filming had been stopped and a dummy put in the actress's place, or that Mr. Méliès used hidden winches and pulleys to propel his actors through the air. A trapdoor allowed them to disappear.

Eventually audiences demanded that their movies have some sort of plot and be more realistic. Special effects became an important area of movie making. But there were few places where a person could train in the special effects field. Anyone who could solve a technical problem immediately became a special effects man. (There have been very few special effects women.) If a particular scene needed a car to dangle over a cliff and some minor employee working on the film could solve the problem of how to do this he might be calling himself a special effects person the next day.

This has all changed today. Special effects men must have two years of propmaking experience plus 1,500 studio hours of training in skills such as propelling spears and arrows, rainmaking, lightning production and cobweb creation. They must also pass a long state exam to receive their powderman's license so they can work with explosives.

Some special effects people today get their training at the movie studios, particularly if members of their family had worked in special effects. A number of today's special effects crews are made up of younger people, many of whom have graduated from college. At the present, when effects mean computerized cameras, rotoscoping, laser animation, hydraulics, and other complicated techniques, a special effects man

Today's special effects—animating a space ship and meteor shower on a three-dimensional multi-plane animation stand.

needs to know something about mechanical engineering, architectural engineering, and various branches of science. In addition, many effects today are still produced by using techniques that date back to the beginning of the film industry, so he must be familiar with the skills used by the older effects men as well. He must know the technicalities and the art of carpentry, lighting, electricity, and plumbing. He must be able to draw his own designs. He must learn to use tools as simple as a needle and thread or as complicated as tomorrow's newest camera. He must be familiar with the possibilities of makeup, although this is art requiring specialists in the field.

The special effects man must also have a vivid imagination for, otherwise, how can he construct things that don't exist? How can he plan the mechanization of huge animals when there are no such animals? How can he plan a Probot for *The Empire Strikes Back* when no such machine has yet been built?

The special effects person must also be prepared to work with almost everyone involved in making the movie. In the beginning, he must work with the director as the sequence of scenes is organized and planned out. He will confer with the art director who designs the scenes and decides how they should appear in the final film. It will be up to the special effects person to carry these suggestions out. To do this, he will have to work with the other departments' staffs, including

Special effects men must have all kinds of skills— Here they work

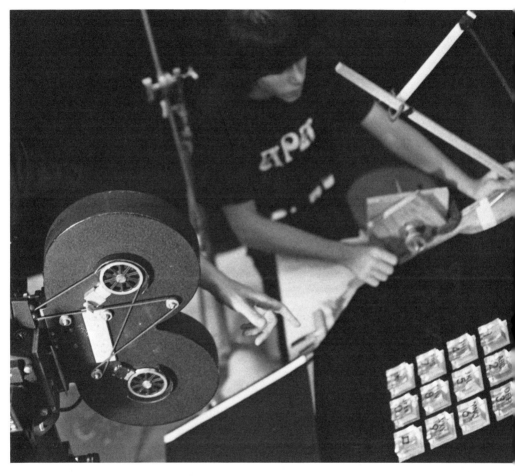

with an oversized replica of a telephone for an AT&T commercial.

carpenters, plasterers, propmakers, painters, and a hundred others. Once the effects are planned, he will have to work with the actors and stuntmen to decide the safest ways of carrying them out. He will have to advise people of the consequences of the effects—will a rock fall in a certain place, will a tree fall a certain way, will an explosive detonate outside a certain area? A special effects man and a director were recently arrested on manslaughter charges in the deaths of three actors, two of them children, in a helicopter explosion stunt that went wrong.

In order to carry out these effects, the crew may work at a movie studio or on location anywhere on the globe. The crew of *Cosmos*, for instance, traveled to Egypt, Holland, Greece, Turkey, India, Germany, Austria, Czechoslovakia, and England. To supervise his work, the special effects man may find himself trudging over a burning desert or up to his hips in snow. He may have to don scuba gear for a deep-sea diving scene in Bermuda, put on mountain climbing gear in Norway, or fly high in the sky for an airplane effect in Australia.

The special effects man has a thousand and one effects to choose from no matter where he is. Usually they can be classified in two areas: *optical* (those that fool the eye) and *mechanical* (those that use some type of motion). Determining which effect will be used in a scene takes an enormous amount of consideration. A *storyboard*—a series of rough sketches showing what will happen in each scene together with a brief description of the dialogue and action—helps the special effects people make their choices.

Special effects may take careful research. For instance, before *The Hindenburg* was filmed, special effects crews spent months traveling all over the world, looking for photographs, blueprints, or even pieces of the real *Hindenburg* before they began building their own airship for filming. They knew the details were important because so many people were still alive who had seen the real airship. The crew working on *Star Wars* spent hours viewing hundreds of dogfight scenes from old war movies. They *spliced* (connected) the best scenes together to make one scene—the gigantic space battle at the end of the movie. For the alien language in the saloon scene, they also spent many hours listening to recordings of languages from all over the world. Thirty or forty were then processed through an electronic synthesizer to form one universal "language."

A special effect can be simple or it can be very complex. For instance, in *Star Wars*, the tiny image of Princess Leia was simply transferred from film to videotape and then back to film to get the eerie flickering effect in the movie. On the other hand, some of the scenes in *2001: A Space Odyssey* used a computer-controlled electronic motion device which moved a

As exact a replica of the Hindenburg as special effects men could make it.

camera in seven different directions to allow special effects people to repeat every move with perfect harmony.

Sometimes more money, more time, and more personnel are spent on special effects than on any other part of the movie or television production. This puts a lot of responsibility on the shoulders of the people who create the effects. The five-minute blast-off in *Destination Moon* took longer to film than all the rest of the movie. The earthquake in the same movie was the focus of the show, so it is not really surprising that it took almost one hundred special effects men working night and day for three months to create it. In *War of the Worlds*, $600,000 was spent to film the live action and $1,400,000 was spent on special effects. In the James Bond movie, *The Spy Who Loved Me*, $40,000 was spent on one prop alone—a tanker that was capable of "gobbling" up three different submarines. And Count Dracula's house in the movie *Dracula* cost more than $100,000. It was used for about a week and a half, then torn down.

This destruction must be particularly hard for the special effects person. He knows that no matter how much time has been spent on the creation of an effect, it may appear for only a split second on the screen, or it may not appear at all. It may be blown up, burned, dropped or otherwise destroyed, or it may be carted away to be stored for some later movie.

All that work going up in pieces.

The special effects person is always ready for the next challenge, however. Will the writer or director be able to stump him this time? Or will he come up with just the right solution to a problem that will have audiences across the country asking, "How did they do that?"

2

SPECIAL EFFECTS PROPS

From huge stage sets to a pistol, from a cream pie destined for someone's face to a huge monster threatening New York, props are all-important. And this is one area where the special effects people really shine.

The effects crew never knows what it will be asked to do. For *The Muppet Movie* they were asked to build a portable diving bell for Muppet controller Jim Henson to operate Kermit as he sat on a log in the middle of a swamp. For the scene showing the Muppets driving cars, real cars were rigged so that a human driver could control the vehicle from the back seat or the trunk. Another effect required *six-foot* custard pies with a mechanical billboard to throw them.

The movie *1941* was another example of a tough assignment. Special effects people had to figure out how to make a periscope on a submarine surface from the water, catch hold of a girl, and carry her about 20 feet into the air. They had to rig a tank to run amok through a paint factory with vats rigged to spill out about 2,500 gallons of paint. A 40mm machine gun had to be fixed to recoil and work its way into a house, destroying it completely. A Christmas tree had to fall over, hit a table, and catapult a bowl of punch through the air up into a chandelier which tips some of the punch onto an unconscious man below. The man awakes and rolls away just as the chandelier crashes to the floor. It took 20 months for the special effects crew to perfect all this.

Props can be made from a variety of materials. The effects people try to keep them inexpensive and light-weight so that they can be easily handled but still look realistic. One of the earliest materials used for props was *papier-mâché* made by soaking newspaper or other paper in water until it became pulp, then adding glue, wheat paste, or liquid. The sticky pulp was then put into a mold, placed over a form or molded by hand, and allowed to dry. It could then be sanded and painted and was sturdy enough for use as furniture. A more modern method is to pour polyurethane plastic foam into a mold. From one to three hours later it is firm enough to be removed and will be so strong it can be sawed, cut, or carved.

A process called *plastic lay-up* is also used. It is the same method used to make surfboards and certain boat or automobile bodies. Plastic lay-up is made by applying a polyester laminating resin over a mold, then applying a glass-fiber cloth, another layer of resin, and so on, until the material is as strong as necessary. Sometimes the cloth is draped over a chicken wire form before the resin is applied. This is the method used to make lightweight rocks.

If a prop is to be broken—perhaps a bottle to be smashed over someone's head—a different material is required. Breakaway props, as they are called, have been constructed of many materials. These range from plaster, pie and bread dough, paraffin, to sugar. When plaster is used, ordinary casting plaster is mixed with sawdust or sand, then poured into a mold or dried and carved. The resulting product crumbles easily at the slightest blow. Baked pie or bread dough breakaways are used if a prop is to be eaten. Bottles and glasses can be made by pouring paraffin into molds and letting them set. Color can be added and dishes and other crockery molded. Glassware, including windows, can be made of sugar dissolved into a small amount of boiling water, but "candy" breakaways are not very realistic. Today, breakaway glassware is also made of plastic which can be purchased ready-made from special supply houses.

Some lightweight props can be made of very light woods such as balsa, used to make model planes and boats. These props do not break as easily as a plaster or plastic breakaway, so they are often broken ahead of time then carefully reassembled, and a dab of glue applied to keep them in one piece until the scene is filmed. Sometimes a piece of black thread or a wire connected to a pin or rod is attached to one piece of the reassembled breakaway. When the thread or wire is pulled, all the pieces fall apart at just the right moment. If an actor is directed to fall *on* a prop, some

This bridge, a breakaway prop, will smash into splinters as the strength of the water is built up to seem to be a raging flood.

spots can be weakened so they will collapse easily. Doors to be broken, or window casings designed to go flying, or rafters and ceilings that should come crashing down on cue are constructed in much the same way.

One of the biggest breakaway props ever was the planet Krypton, birthplace of Superman. In the movie, the huge planet was assembled from separate pieces of plastic and fiberglass. A hydraulic machine was rigged under the set to create the earthquake that triggers the destruction of the planet, which easily fell to pieces.

The same movie also featured a model of the Golden Gate Bridge. It was very delicately made because the effects men didn't want to have to use powerful explosives to break the model up. It was carefully tacked together, and every time a big wind came along everyone rushed outside to see if it was still standing. A terrible storm did finally cause the bridge to collapse. Fortunately, all the shots had already been taken.

Of course, not all props are breakaway props. Some are quite sturdy and can range in size from the smallest magical thimble to the largest piece of furniture. It is the large, oversized props which create the biggest stir. For instance, in *Tom Thumb* the main character was supposed to be $5\frac{1}{2}$ inches tall. To make him seem small, all the props around him had to be very large. The props for some of the sets included a 16-foot top hat, an 80-foot cobbler's bench, and a 55-foot baby's cradle. In *Fantastic Voyage*, a group of scientists are reduced in size so they can travel through the bloodstream of a patient to perform delicate brain surgery. Special effects crews fashioned huge body parts from styrofoam. The heart was 15 feet long, 5 feet high and 7 feet across. The brain was 5 *million* times larger than a real brain, and one eye was 17 feet long and 5 feet high.

Building a miniature prop can be just as difficult. It takes lots of time and patience, as anyone who has ever put together a model airplane knows. But in the movies and television, miniature props often save a lot of time and money.

When building a miniature, the special effects men must be very careful to keep everything exactly to scale, in proportion to the real thing. If the model is even a fraction of an inch off, the whole scene can appear out of proportion. Nothing in the background can be allowed to detract from the miniature, for even something as small as an insect can look like a flying monster next to the tiny models.

Even though the word "miniature" makes us think of something very small, miniatures made for movies and television can also be very large and detailed. The

She towers over an entire city.

difference is that the miniatures are still not as big as the things they represent. The city in *Battlestar Galactica*, for example, was some 100 yards long, very large for a miniature city but of course not as big as the real thing would be. The Golden Gate Bridge in *Superman* had a span of 60 feet—approximately 6 stories high if laid on end, but it was small compared to the 4,200-foot span of the real thing. Miniature vehicles were used to make the bridge look still bigger. The largest, a bus, was actually only three feet long. Superman (Christopher Reeve) was shown flying towards the bridge, but he was really a long way from the miniature. When shown on film, however, the whole scene looked very realistic.

On the other hand, miniatures can look enormous on the screen when in fact they are actually very small. Some of the 45 fighters and starships made for *Battlestar Galactica* were no bigger than 11 inches. The battlestar itself was only 6 feet and weighed only 60 pounds. Made entirely out of model kits from the hobby stores, the minute details and controlled lighting used by the special effects men made it seem gigantic and awe-inspiring.

If a miniature is going to be seen from a distance, it can be as simple as a flat cutout. But for those scenes with close-ups, the miniature must be as realistic as possible for today's sophisticated audiences. Many of

A street in miniature. The alley for the TV series, "The Greatest

American Hero."

the miniatures are very detailed, therefore, and often have movable parts. The miniature of the airship *Hindenburg* included moving motors, elevators, and rudders and working running lights. The ship could even dump water used as ballast to lighten its imaginary load. A miniature amusement park in *1941* included tiny amusement rides, tiny delicatessen items placed in store windows, tiny menus waiting for imaginary customers, and tiny pinball machines in an arcade. The streets were even littered with tiny newspapers telling of the attack on Pearl Harbor, the subject of the movie.

Action props are usually designed to move in some way—perhaps by controls from the back seat like the cars in *The Muppet Movie,* or by electrical wiring inside, as with some robots. Hydraulic equipment can also be used to move some props. In *Superman,* the hero is supposed to push a huge rock off a mountain. The mountain and rocks were miniature, but even so they were very heavy. The rock was about eight feet high and weighed half a ton. Superman was placed on a platform behind the rock. He pretended to push the rock, and a hydraulic machine actually did the work.

Action props are a very useful way to depict living creatures. The simplest type is some sort of costume with a real person inside. C-3PO and Chewbacca from the *Star Wars* movies were real people inside costumes. The Ewoks in *Return of the Jedi* were midgets

One way for a ship to move across an "ocean." This one is from
Raise the Titanic.

and small children from three to four feet tall in plastic, latex, and fur suits.

Another way to make lifelike creatures is to actually film a real animal, like a lizard, and add a miniature scene later. This is how they filmed *Journey to the Center of the Earth* when they wanted the hero to encounter giant reptilian-type monsters.

Other "creature" props have consisted of miniature clay models photographed one frame at a time. This is called animation or stop action. Animation may be combined with live action. For example, a model, say a dinosaur, is placed in one position in the scene. A single frame of film is exposed, then the model is moved just a fraction of an inch and another frame is exposed, and so on. When the model appears on film, it seems to be moving. Examples on television are Gumby and Mr. Bill from the *Saturday Night Live* show. The most famous movie example is probably the great ape, King Kong. Unfortunately, the results of using this process are often jerky and unnatural, especially when seen on the old movies. New techniques, such as a process called go-motion, have helped make animation more realistic. Camera men use computers to move cameras and creatures at the same time for a much smoother effect. Go-motion was used in the bicycle-riding scene in *E.T. The Extra-Terrestrial*, when the outer space creature and his new friends ride off into the sky.

Another way of imitating live creatures is to use a life-size replica of the creature itself and operate it mechanically. Robby, the robot in *Forbidden Planet*, contained 2,600 feet of electrical wiring that flashed lights, spun antennae, and whirled gadgets inside his transparent head. R2D2 in *Star Wars* ran on a similar principle, but was much more sophisticated and realistic. Mechanized replicas of gnats, ants, scorpions, spiders, praying mantises, giant turtles, flying horses, vultures, and many other movie animals have tried to take over the world at one time or another. It is sometimes difficult to tell the real from the fake, especially when they are combined. In *Raiders of the Lost Ark*, live snakes and fake snakes were used for a really chilling effect.

The final type of action prop consists of a hand puppet. This is one of the most popular ways today of depicting living creatures thanks to puppeteers like Jim Henson and Frank Oz. Some examples in recent movies are Yoda and the evil sluglike Java in *The Empire Strikes Back*. These creatures were actually combinations of clay, aluminum tubing, steel rods, latex, and vinyl air hoses. Air sacks, paddles, and valves like those used on Michael Jackson's face in *Thriller* were used to make the creatures appear more real. It took six men to operate the mechanical insides of Java

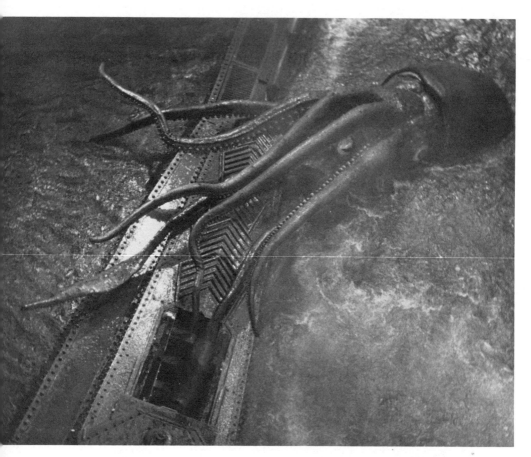

Mechanical animals are a favorite of special effects people.

A giant squid attacks a submarine in "Twenty Thousand Leagues Under The Sea."

Robot prop.

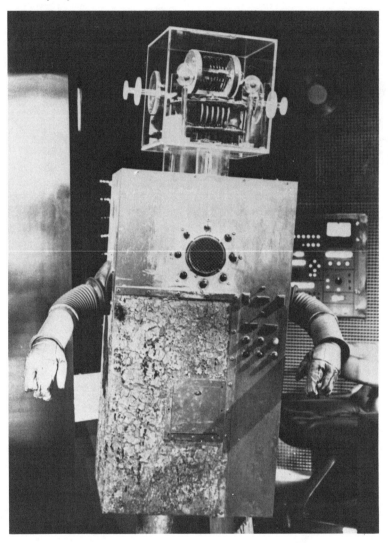

Puppet soldiers manipulated by special effects men prepare for battle in "Bedknobs and Broomsticks."

Special effects men put the finishing touches on the face of an actor being filmed in a commercial for the game "Aliens" manufactured by Milton Bradley.

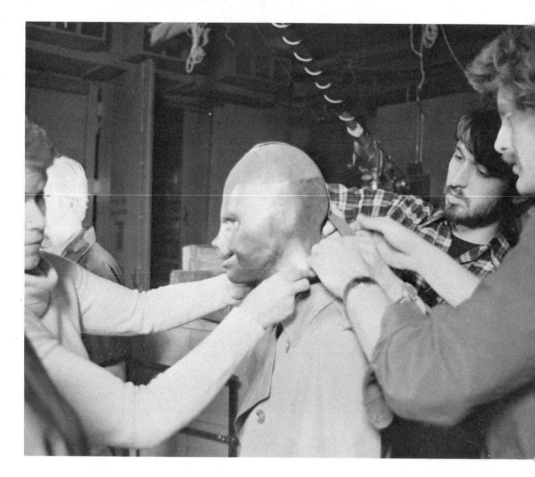

from his giant, swinging tail to his flaring nostrils and bulging eyes. Two tons of clay and 600 pounds of laytex made up the outside.

Bruce, the shark used in the movie *Jaws*, was actually many different models. One model was made for full-face views, one for the left side, and one for the right. Inside were electronic gears to run the huge models. They traveled underwater, sometimes on tracks, at other times manipulated by mechanical arm and pulley systems. Since seawater corroded plastic skin, Bruce's skin had to be replaced each week. Each model also had two sets of teeth, one of steel for realistic scenes and one of rubber for the time when Bruce worked with actors. Bruce was used for almost every shark scene in the movie. One exception was when the shark expert played by Richard Dreyfuss was threatened by a great white shark while underwater. For this scene a real shark was used and a midget stuntman took the actor's place to make the shark look bigger.

A number of E.T.s were used for *E.T.* One was a lightweight electro-mechanical E.T. that was capable of thirty facial movements and thirty body movements. A more complicated E.T. was built for close-ups. He was electronic and had eighty-six separate movements. (King Kong had only forty.) A third E.T. was a costume worn by little people for scenes where

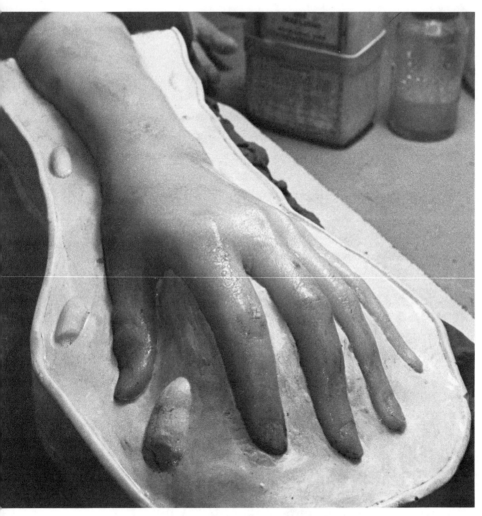

A close-up of the anatomical casting of an automated hand
to be used in a toy commercial.

A model monster, this one from *King Kong.*

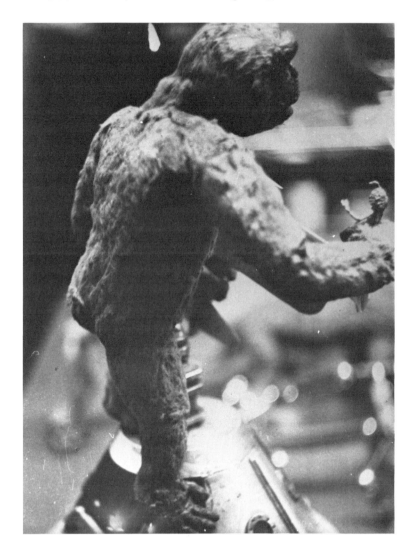

E.T. was shown walking. A number of simpler rubber suits were also worn by little people for the opening scenes when E.T. is running through the forest. All the E.T. heads could be removed and put on different models. There were four models of heads, radio-controlled or electronic. When a close-up was needed, the operators would take off a radio-controlled head and replace it with an electronic one that was capable of more movement around the forehead, lips, eyes, eyebrows, and tongue. It took two men just to operate the lips and tongue and obviously they had to work together very closely. During filming, one accidentally stuck out the tongue while the other closed the mouth—and E.T. bit his tongue!

3

SPECIAL EFFECTS TECHNIQUES

There are certain techniques available to the special effects person that allow him to carry out his assignment creatively. The way the camera is handled, the way the film is controlled, the various ideas involved in using accessories, like mirrors or wires, to fool the human eye—these are all part of the bag of tricks the special effects person carries.

One of the earliest methods used to fool the eye was the *glass shot*. The glass shot allows the special effects person to add things to a scene that aren't really there. For instance, clouds can be added to a cloudless sky or more stories can be added to an existing building. To do this, a camera is set up in front of a live scene. A sheet of glass is placed two or three feet in front of the camera. Checking and rechecking the live scene through his camera viewfinder, the artist sketches an outline of the details he wants to add. Then he paints them in to blend perfectly with the existing scene. In *Butch Cassidy and the Sundance Kid*, for instance, when the heroes jump off a cliff into a river to escape the posse, the cliff was added on glass. In *Superman*, special effects artists used about 30 glass shots, including painted skies, an atom bomb explosion, and Superman's view of earth.

Another way of adding details to a scene is by using a *matte shot*. Although there are several ways of creating such a shot, one of the simplest is to put a black card called a *matte card* in the camera and expose the film. The exposed film is then taken out of the camera and put aside without being processed. A few feet of test film which had already been shot and developed are placed in the camera. This test film is then projected on a piece of glass that has been covered with white tempera paint. This is called a *matte board*. A matte painter paints the picture on the glass and the background is covered with black paint. The exposed undeveloped film which had previously been put aside is now replaced in the camera and shot. The resulting picture is a composite of live-action film and painting. Matte paintings were used extensively throughout *The Empire Strikes Back*, in some of the snow scenes, Cloud City scenes, and Bog Planet scenes. A lot of matte paintings were used at the end of the film when Darth Vader and Luke fight a laser sword battle inside a giant tube on a catwalk. Luke's fall down the tube was also done with mattes. In *The Black Hole*, 150 matte shots were used. Many of them were needed to create the impression that the ship, the *Cygnus*, was 1,000 feet long when it was really only 70 feet.

Matte shots are one of the chief methods for making a scene seem as if it is some place it isn't. For instance, in *Cosmos*, a Los Angeles golf course was turned into medieval England by adding a complete Gothic cathedral on glass. It was so realistic, people back at the studio were unable to tell glass shots had

A miniature replica of the beautiful Alexandrian Library built for

the PBS series "Cosmos." Dr. Carl Sagan was later shot on blue and matted in to the miniature.

been used. In *Close Encounters of the Third Kind* the final scene was supposedly located in Wyoming. In reality, it was shot in a huge blimp hangar in Mobile, Alabama. Some frames for this scene contained 50 or more individual shots brought together. One frame might include the huge UFO, the horizon, the terrain, stars (drawn in), a lighting effect or two, and several other matte shots.

Another way to fool the eye is to animate a scene by drawing in the characters the way it is done in cartoons. For instance, in *Mary Poppins*, the main characters, played by Julie Andrews and Dick Van Dyke, worked on an almost empty stage. In the movie, when you see them stepping on the backs of turtles, they are actually stepping on black pipes on the set. The turtles and scenery were drawn in separately, using animation.

In addition to changing or adding to the live scene, another way of fooling the eye is to manipulate the film and camera. The camera speed can be slowed down or speeded up. The amount of light allowed into the camera can be changed. Front or rear projection can be used. In *rear projection*, the camera and projector face each other. A screen is placed between them, and the image is focused on the screen from the projector and photographed by the camera. *Front screen projection,* on the other hand, is simply projecting the image onto a screen and rephotographing it there. The camera in this case is placed next to the

One of the special cameras and projectors used to make miniature sets realistic.

Another view of equipment used to make this village look life-like.

projector. The camera and projector are aligned until the picture on the screen fills the camera's viewfinder, at which time it is photographed.

One machine particularly helpful to special effects people is the *optical printer*. This is a movie projector and process camera facing each other. A master positive is placed in the projector and the process camera contains a negative. As one frame of the master positive is projected, one frame of the negative is exposed. In this way, copies can be made of a film and a variety of effects created. For example, by adjusting the relative speeds of camera and projector, one can get slow motion, frame freezing, and reverse action. If you use a black and white negative, you can convert color to black and white. Other effects that can be gotten with the optical printer are enlargement or reduction of details, converting day photography into night and many others.

The special effects person must also be an expert in lighting. The 68-foot V'ger model in *Star Trek: The Motion Picture*, for instance, looked much more futuristic because of the use of neon tubes, fiber optics, and lasers. In *Close Encounters of the Third Kind*, sophisticated fiber optics and light-scanning techniques were used to control and color the light on the film, creating shapes where no shapes actually existed. And the "ship of the imagination" in *Cosmos* owed its existence to some 250 lighting instruments controlled by computer.

Small explosions and light rays give a realistic appearance to

the laser battle from "The Black Hole."

Dr. Carl Sagan gazes out over the props that special lighting

effects make so dramatic in "Cosmos."

Early magicians knew the value of using mirrors to fool their audiences and special effects people were quick to borrow this tool. For instance, mirrors were used to shoot one of the sea battles in the 1934 version of *Cleopatra*. The scene was supposed to show more than 35 galleys at battle. There were actually only two miniature galleys, but mirrors placed all around the set made it seem like a whole fleet. Today, mirrors are still used. For instance, in *Cosmos*, when they wanted to show a locomotive crashing into the camera lens, they placed a mirror on the tracks and the camera safely off to the side. Although it looks as if the locomotive is coming straight toward the camera, it is actually crashing into the mirror.

Mirrors have also been the props used for many of the ghosts that have appeared in movies and television over the years. Usually a partially transparent mirror is placed at an angle in front of the camera. The image of a person standing off to one side is picked up and superimposed on the scene being filmed. The image in the mirror becomes the shadowy ghost in the film.

Ghosts, angels, superheroes, Peter Pan, Mary Poppins, and others have been propelled through the air by means of another important piece of special effects equipment—wire. Piano wire is usually used because when managed correctly, it can be very strong—strong enough, in fact, to hold a car teetering dangerously on the edge of a cliff. The wires which are used to fly actors are attached to a crane overhead. The actors can spend as long as two hours in the air for just two seconds of film and sometimes run the risk of accidentally crashing into nearby scenery or props. All this may change with a new system developed by special effects wizards for *Superman*. They made up a plastic body mold and attached it on top of a 40-foot high hydraulically-powered pole. For flying, the actor is placed, stomach down on the mold. The pole carries mold and actor along runners. Clothing hides the mold and the pole is not shown.

Sometimes the special effects man needs to convince his audience that something *doesn't* exist. This is especially necessary in the many movies that feature invisible heroes like *Harvey*, whose main character was a giant invisible rabbit, or *The Invisible Man*, filmed in the 1930s. Many ingenious ideas were employed to show things that weren't really there. For instance, when police chase the invisible man, they are able to trace him because they can see his footprints in the snow. Special effects men needed to figure out how to make footprints when no one was walking over the area. They dug a trench, covered it with a board which already had footprints cut out and reattached the cutouts with pegs. The whole thing was covered with plastic snow. A hidden rope pulled the pegs loose when the invisible man supposedly ran by.

Modern machinery often replaces more old-fashioned wires for flying sequences. In "The Greatest American Hero," the suspended camera shoots the actor in a flying harness against a blue background. It will later be composited with the traveling shot of the alley shown on pp. 34–35.

The footprint cutouts dropped out, snow filled the holes and made footprints.

At the end of the movie, when the invisible man supposedly dies, special effects men needed to show him slowly reappearing. Audiences saw the impression of his body in the mattress and pillow, then his skeleton, then the rest of his body. This was done by making a pillow out of plaster and sheets of papier-mâché. Then the indentation of the invisible man was added. The camera filmed the mattress and pillow, then stopped. A real skeleton was added and filmed. Than a series of dummies, each with additional parts of the body, were filmed. Many of these techniques are still used today in movies such as *Heaven Can Wait* and *Oh, God*.

4

ATMOSPHERIC EFFECTS

One problem the special effects man faces is providing weather conditions. For instance, if a scene is to be shot in the fog, it would be ridiculous and costly to wait around for a foggy day. It would be much more practical to provide the fog artificially.

In early films, mist and fog were created by spraying mineral oil into the air. Unfortunately the oil also created a fine mist on the actors' clothes and made the floor very slippery and dangerous. Eventually, cameras used *fog filters*, pieces of specially treated ground glass, to give a foggy effect. Today machines are available which provide an oil-based fog ranging in variety from drifting fogs to low-hanging fogs or hazes. But fog filters are still used and range from a slight mist to dense fog. However, they are motionless and therefore unlike real fog and mist, which move. So they are saved mostly for close-ups.

A foggy effect can be produced simply by placing a folded white gauzelike material over the camera lens. Bee smokers, devices used by bee keepers to quiet the bees so they won't sting, have also been used to create a light fog or haze. Dry ice in water is good for creating low-hanging ground fog. It is made in large containers called "rumble pots." Unfortunately, the rumble pot can't be used when sound is being recorded because, as the name implies, it makes loud rumbles and hisses.

Special effects produce the fog that rolls in on the scene for
a commercial for the game "Aliens" produced by Milton
Bradley.

No matter what method is used to make fog, it is very difficult to keep it consistent over a long period of time and takes a great deal of patience to get it just right.

Many of the same methods used to make fog can also be used to make smoke or haze. In addition, a combination of chemicals called "liquid smoke" is also used. This is the same product skywriters use to spell out their aerial messages. When smoke is needed, a valve of the tank is opened and the liquid streams out. When small puffs of smoke are needed, in battle scenes, for instance, the liquid smoke is bottled in thin glass Christmas tree balls, then sealed with wax. The bulb is thrown and when it shatters, smoke appears in just the right spot. It can also be used to show smoke and steam from a sinking ship, the smoldering coals of a campfire, or the dying embers of a burned building. It can even be used for the steam in a cup of hot coffee or soup, although it could never be consumed—liquid smoke is extremely poisonous.

Another problem special effects men face is providing rain on cue. If the movie or television production is being filmed outside, fire hoses can be aimed into the air. For a really ferocious storm, a wind machine can be used to blow the rain at a slant. Lightning can be added by using a light machine with shutters. Opening and closing the shutters allows the light to flash through, just as Morse code was sent between ships. Pyrotechnics—fireworks—although more dangerous, are also handy to show effects like lightning striking a tree. A flash sheet, a thin piece of material, is sprinkled with explosive flash powder and rolled into strips. The strips are mounted on an adhesive tape and stuck onto the tree. They are then set off by an electronic signal, making it look as if the tree has been struck by lightning.

When filming inside, water pipes are often installed overhead to provide artificial rain. When using these pipes, it is necessary to spread a large sheet of plastic over the floor and turn it up at the edges to contain the water. Otherwise the floor and equipment would be ruined, and it would take hours to clean up the mess.

If the rain is supposed to turn into hail according to the script, small white beans or white plastic beads can be let loose from above. Sometimes plastic bits from plastic salvage or reprocessing plants are also used.

If the hail turns to snow, the director must decide if he or she wants falling snow or if the snow is to be used as a set dressing. A set dressing can be a ground cover, clinging snow, or drifts and chunks. Such strange materials as bleached cornflakes, shredded asbestos, chopped feathers, balsa chips, and soap flakes have all been used to simulate falling snow. Even the little paper circles left over after punching holes in notebook paper have been rescued from book

A machine provides the atmosphere of steam for a

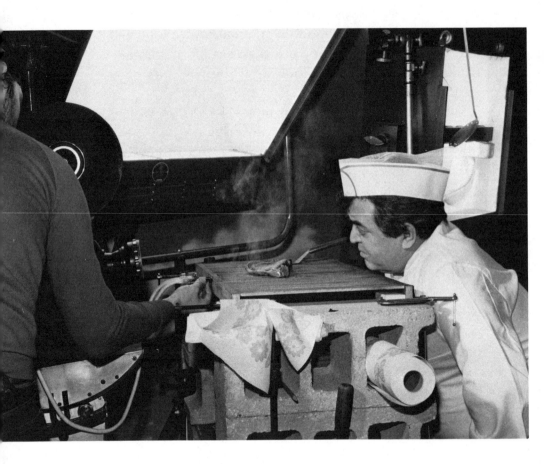

commercial for Ball Park Franks.

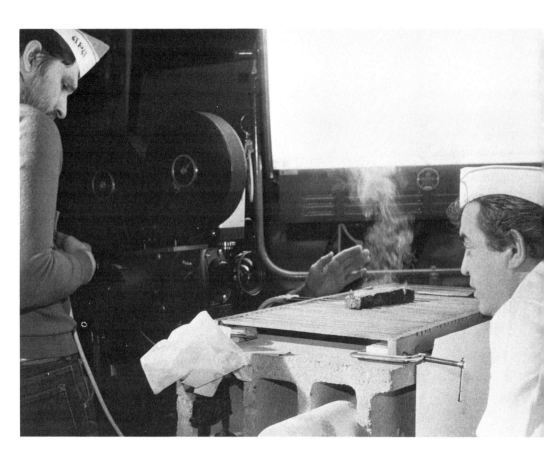

binderies and paper factories to appear in movies as snow. Today, a lot of studios also use shredded polyethylene bags similar to, but a little heavier than, the clothes bags used at the cleaners. When the bags are pounded into pulp, they become pure white and look amazingly like snow. Plastic snowflakes can also be bought, not only in different sizes but in pastel colors as well.

Snow machines may also be used to create snow. The machines are usually a long, deep hopper with an opening along the bottom. They are run by a small electric motor which governs the rate at which the snow sifts through and can provide a slight snowfall or a blizzard. Wind machines and large sieves can also distribute the snow on the set.

Not all the materials used for falling snow are suitable for use as a set dressing. Most are very light and are easily displaced by the slightest breeze or movement. Heavier or stickier materials such as ground-up styrofoam, limerock, and perlite can be substituted. The salt used in ice cream makers and water softeners can also provide glistening snow when necessary.

Clinging snow needed to stick to sets is usually applied by spreading a foaming chemical snow with a fire hose nozzle. The same snow used to decorate Christmas trees is also used as set dressing. If a director wants a scene to be truly realistic, the special effects man can make real snow. He uses an ice-crushing machine and spraying equipment similar to that used by trucking and railroad companies for icing the insides of refrigerator cars. This snow is not only expensive, but it melts, is hard to clean up, and has to be used on a refrigerated set. Of course, for true realism the cast and crew can go over to Norway as in the filming of *The Empire Strikes Back*. Usually, however, it is very difficult to film in large areas covered with snow because of the glare.

Ice floes large enough to support actors can be made by fastening empty oil drums together like a raft and covering them with plastic. For small amounts of ice, melted paraffin is poured slowly onto water. Icicles are made by dipping cellophane strips into the melted paraffin or dripping the paraffin over forms cut in the shape of icicles. Icicles may also be bought in various lengths from special supply houses.

Frost can be applied by using a solution of Epsom salts in very stale beer. Prismatic lacquer may also be used for frost. The lacquer, found in some paint stores, is applied with a fine brush and allowed to dry slowly.

Sometimes a combination of atmospheric effects create a certain climate. For a UFO scene in *Cosmos*, for instance, rain machines, fog machines and light machines were all used. The alien craft was created by putting a heavy fog machine in front of lights. Close-ups of the actors, who were supposed to see the UFO while traveling in the rain, were filmed with rain on the windows while flashing lights off stage gave the impression of street lamps and passing vehicles.

What atmospheric effects would you use when filming something like *Cosmos* to picture the "ship of the imagination" traveling on a ten-billion-light-year journey from the edge of the universe? How would you simulate a Milky Way for instance? You know what it looks like from Earth but how would it look coming from another direction? Special effects people working on *Cosmos* consulted available scientific data about the size and shape of the Milky Way and got enough information for a pretty good idea of what it looked like. Then they were able to combine stop-motion photography with optical printer techniques and animation to create a galaxy. Live-action models were put in front of beautiful paintings of space. Smoke and fog were used to show the atmosphere and dust storms around the planets. One technique required the director to breathe heavily on a special mirror used to show the spaceship flying in and out of the clouds!

We know how a windblown cape would look on earth, but what if you had to show that cape being blown around in the sky? This was the problem in *Superman*. Superman's cape had a tendency to swirl under him instead of flying out behind. The solution was to devise a mechanical system which Christopher Reeve (Superman) could wear as a body pack.

It was radio controlled and could be used under any conditions, whether he was flying at night by wires around the back lot or on a stage using the new hydraulic rig.

How would you create a black hole in outer space, showing the collection of gas and stellar trash that orbits around its perimeter, color and temperature changes, and magnetic lines of force around the hole? This was the task of Dov Jacobson and Judy Kreijanovsky for the movie *The Black Hole*. These two special effects people have their own company called Cartoon Kitchen. They mulled over suggestions ranging from spinning paintings at acute angles to flushing ink down the toilet. They finally decided simply to use animation to produce the required effects.

Stars seen from earth are millions of miles away. But what if a spaceship was cruising through those stars? What would they look like then? Scientific data has proven they would be very, very bright. For *The Black Hole*, special effects people used a dark backing with thousands of holes punched in it with 1,250,000 watts of light shining through. This gave off so much heat that they had only two minutes to shoot the scene. Then the lights had to be turned off or the heat would set off the sprinkler system. The company had to have a fireman on the set to tell them when it was cool enough to shoot.

Unfortunately for the special effects team, scientific

Dr. Carl Sagan uses props of the different planets. Newly-discovered facts must be incorporated into all the models.

knowledge is changing so rapidly that it is almost impossible to keep up. When the special effects team of *Cosmos* was preparing a model of Venus, new data was received showing that the atmosphere was somewhat dense at the surface, and the planet was surrounded by cloud layers and there were about 25 flashes of lightning per second. Right in the middle of building their model they had to stop and start over. They finally injected chemicals along with a large amount of milk into a tank of water to produce the cloudy effect. The colors of the clouds were selected by computers that matched scientific data with color chips.

5

EXPERIMENTING WITH SPECIAL EFFECTS AT HOME

Many experts in the special effects field today began experimenting while they were still in grade school. Steven Spielberg was shooting war movies at a nearby Air Force base while he was still in elementary school! Rick Baker, responsible for the gruesome makeup on the 30 ghouls in Michael Jackson's *Thriller* video, began making up his friends at age 10. He used common household products to fake burns and horrible body scars.

You can begin experimenting at home too with everyday things around the house to make movies with a simple home movie or video camera. There's fake blood, for instance. A prime ingredient in any war or horror movie, it can be bought from most theatrical supply stores. But it is much more fun and usually more economical to make at home. Even professional moviemakers have used everything from automotive transmission fluid to chocolate syrup for blood. You can probably come up with your own formula by experimenting. You could use milk thickened with flour and colored with red dye. You could use Karo corn syrup thickened with flour and colored with red dye, or use cocoa with water and red coloring. For blood clots, you could use red Jello added to red food coloring. For some really gross effects, dip tissue paper into the Jello before it is completely set. Twist the tissue paper until it is long and stringy. The results look

A special effects man begins a plastic "face" for the filming of a commercial for "Wizards," a game produced by Milton Bradley.

like intestines or other grisly innards. If you want to show abrasions on the skin, spread a little kitchen cleanser on the actor's skin. Then sprinkle a few drops of watered-down ketchup on the cleanser. The important thing to keep in mind when experimenting with making blood is to be sure you have the right consistency and color for the scene you are shooting.

Usually stage blood is put on the actor in between takes. You can apply yours with a brush or eyedropper for the best effects. Allow it to run down the face, arm or whatever. Just be sure to let it set a little before filming to make it look more realistic. If you want your actor to bleed on camera, you will have to use some type of sack device. Real special effects men use blood sacks that are broken with small, electrically detonated explosive charges called "bullet hits," but this is very dangerous and not to be used by anyone except professionals. It is much safer and just as much fun to experiment with things found around the house. For instance, you can make a blood sack by pouring your blood recipe into plastic sandwich bags or thin toy balloons. Use a funnel or basting syringe. Twist the top and put a rubber band around it. The actor can then hold the blood sack in his or her hand so that it is hidden from the camera. Or it could be hidden under clothes. At the right time, the actor grabs his or her "wound" and the blood sack breaks. Remember: almost any recipe you think up will probably stain

Painting on the wounds of war.

clothing, so use very old costumes or you will have a very irritated parent. And be sure ingredients won't harm skin or eyes.

Experimenting with props is also fun for beginners. One of the easiest props to create at home is rocks. For moon rocks or small asteroids all you need are some Earth rocks. Be sure to pick out some that are shiny and some that are dull, for variety. If they are to be asteroids, you can suspend them by fishing line, and place in front of a star background. Or you can attach the fishing line to sticks and have friends jiggle them, with the dangling "asteroids," in front of the camera.

Space rocks can also be made of tinfoil. Crumple a large piece up until it is a loosely packed ball. The surface will look sharp and bumpy. Flatten the bottom so that it won't roll around while you are filming. Finish with adhesive spray, found at craft stores, and then sprinkle with sand. You can spray paint it beige or gray and place it on your set. By the way, Ovaltine breakfast drink makes a great futuristic alien planet surface if you are doing science fiction.

For something bigger, like mountains, take three or four sheets of ordinary paper. Glue the upper part of each one so you can paste one on top of the other to make a pulpy flat "plate." Wet and crumple and crease it into mountains, craters, hills, and valleys. Then glue the landscape to a piece of cardboard or plywood. You can add sheets of paper, molding them as you go along for more peaks and craters. Then you can paint your scene with tempera paints.

Styrofoam is another favorite material to use for anything from bricks to boulders because it is lightweight and easily carved into shapes. To make a boulder, for instance, you can glue several sections of styrofoam together to get one big block. Then you can cut, carve, gouge, beat, and dent it until it looks like a boulder. You could paint it beige or dark gray. You might want to add a little moss—found at craft or flower stores—for a very realistic effect.

Another type of boulder can be made out of scrap wood and wire screening if you are handy with tools. It wouldn't be as light as styrofoam, but it is cheaper. All you need are some scrap pieces of lightweight wood. Nail them together to make a cube as big as you want your boulder. You can then nail or staple pieces of cardboard or smaller pieces of wood to round the shape somewhat. Staple metal window screening on and shape it into the kind of boulder shape you want. (You will need to wear gloves while working with the screening.) Soak paper towels in a paste of flour and water. You can add a little white glue like Elmer's to the flour and water to give it more body. Soak each towel in the paste mixture. Carefully press out extra water and apply it to the boulder form. When it is completely dry, paint the boulder beige or gray.

Everyday props like tables and chairs can be made of cardboard if you don't have any old furniture you can use. Cardboard is free—usually. You can find it at furniture stores or supermarkets. You might have your parents help you cut the cardboard with a wood saw or knife. Then glue the pieces together just like furniture. The only drawback about cardboard is that it will not be a breakable prop. But it can be painted and will look real enough on screen. Or cover it with contact paper that is made to look like wood.

Breakaway props like plates, cups, saucers, and other dishes can be made out of bread or pie dough. Make up some dough using almost any recipe from a cookbook and shape it to look like the dish you want. Bake the props according to the recipe and then paint or color them with food dye.

The important thing to remember when using any breakaway prop is that even though these items are meant to "break away," they still can send chips or pieces flying and this can be dangerous. Be very careful when using them on anything or anybody.

Once you have your props prepared, you might want to experiment with some atmospheric effects for your scenes. Going for the scary effect? Cobwebs are a must, and although you could buy or rent a web spinner from almost any theatrical supply house, it's more fun and cheaper to make cobwebs at home. One easy way is to take two 4- by 10-inch pieces of cardboard and place a layer of rubber cement on one side of both pieces. Press them firmly together for about 20 seconds. Then slowly pull them apart. The long thin strands of the rubber cement will string apart. Scrape the strands off the cardboard and attach them to furniture or to each other for the desired pattern. (Be sure it is your old, cheap prop furniture and not Mom's good living room set.)

Going for the frosty scene? It's fun to experiment with snow other than just at Christmastime. If you know someone who works at a company with computers, ask if you have the paper confetti produced by computer-card punching. When you have enough to shoot your scene, have someone climb a ladder—carefully—and toss the paper dots all over the sets.

For smaller scenes, like miniatures, you can use styrofoam to make snow drifts. White sawdust is also good. You can add a little silver glitter to make it sparkle like new-fallen snow. Icicles can be made by twisting pieces of plastic wrap and dipping them in melted candle wax (with adult supervision). When they harden, you will be able to hang them up. Candle wax can also be used to make little ice patches. Drip the wax onto hot water in a bucket. It will harden into a sheet or puddle of "ice." Be *very* careful—candle wax is hot.

If you have an old aquarium at home, you can make some really neat surrealistic clouds like those in *Close*

Encounters of the Third Kind. Put the aquarium some place where there will be room for a little set in front of it. Fill the tank with water and wait for it to settle. You might add a background behind the tank like a piece of colored paper or some artwork. Put a light on each side of the tank and maybe one in the back if you wish. You can also add a miniature set in front of the tank. Now you are ready to make your clouds.

You need a basting syringe from the kitchen or you can use a short hose or section of pipe to put the liquid in the tank. The liquid can be a thick mixture of liquid tempera paints. You can buy dry tempera at a craft store and experiment by adding water until you get the right consistency. You can also use milk dyed with food coloring or clothing dyes bought at the store. Fill the basting syringe, pipe, or hose with the liquid. Squirt the liquid into the tank. Begin filming as the liquid swirls its way through the water. Presto! You have some great moving clouds.

An easy way to add rain to your set is to take a small styrofoam tray like the ones meat comes in from the supermarket, and punch small holes in it. Fill the tray with silver glitter. When you are ready to start filming, shake the tray and you get instant rain that won't leave your set all wet and soggy.

Stars can be made from a large piece of black bristol board, available at a hobby store. Punch tiny holes all over with a pin. Put a light behind the board far enough away so it doesn't heat up the board—and you have a sky full of tiny stars. If you put window screening over the lens of the camera, far enough away to keep it from damaging the lens, the stars will appear pointed.

The secret to special effects at home is to use your imagination. Look around the craft or hobby stores or hardware stores for just the right material to make the special effects you need. Even professional special effects people use everyday items for multi-million-dollar movies. You can add to your knowledge by studying films that use a lot of special effects and by reading every book you can find on the subject. Practice is the key to creating really good special effects in your home films.

INDEX

ABOUT THE AUTHOR

Shaaron Cosner is an Air Force "brat," educated in many countries around the world, finally settling down in Arizona where she received a bachelor's degree in English at Arizona State University. She became a newspaper reporter and freelance writer, and is the author of five other books for young people. Ms. Cosner, her husband, son and daughter make their home in Tempe, Arizona.